18 HOLES OF A CLUB GOLFER

Duncan McCarthy

Thanks to those who have truly supported the journey so far. Your love, passion and guidance are priceless and I look forward to more great things to come.

Copyright © 2014 by Duncan McCarthy

No reproduction without permission from the author.
All rights reserved.

ISBN-13: 978-1499268508

INTRODUCTION

"Just play, have fun, enjoy the game"

Michael Jordan

Since beginning my journey I have been fortunate to work with golfers of all abilities, from club level golfers through to golfers who have competed at the highest level, golfers from 11 years of age through to the senior golfer. As much as I have helped them with their performance they have also taught me things at the same time.

Anyone who has worked with me over a period of time is surprised at the simplicity of how I deliver my work. What I always remember is that a golfer is just trying to put a little white ball into a hole in the least amount of shots.

My role ultimately comes down to getting the golfer out of their own way and trust themselves. How I do this changes from individual to individual. We are all wired differently and therefore what works for one may not work for another.

You can help a golfer on the surface no problem and many coaches do this which is great but my personal belief is to start from within first. There are many golfers at all levels who convey strength on the outside but internally they are fragile when faced with a challenge. I call them egg shell golfers.

My main goal with this book is to offer club level, and even beyond, golfers a quick reference guide to some common phrases and situations that come up in a round of golf. It is not to complicate your time out on the course but in fact simplify how you think, which in turn will allow your game to flow.

I hope you enjoy the book and refer to it regularly to keep the most important club in your bag relaxed, clear and calm.

CONTENTS

18 HOLES OF A CLUB GOLFER

"Don't go left"	10
"Get it inside a bucket lid"	13
"I must hole this"	16
"This lie is awful"	18
"I hate this game"	21
"I hate this club"	24
"I must hit this hard"	26
"I hit it great in practice"	28
"I haven't got time to practice"	31
"I was fine until the halfway house"	34
"I missed so many putts today"	38
"Come on let's hit a good first tee shot"	40
"I'm always rushing to the first tee"	43
"This is my bogey hole"	47
"Whoever put those pins out today wants shooting"	50
"I've got the wrong club, I better hit it though"	53
"I can't believe I missed that last putt"	56
"It should have been 72"	59
Duncan's Do's	61
About the Author	62

"I always like to see a person stand up to a golf ball as though he were perfectly at home in its presence."

Bobby Jones

1. "Don't go left"

You're on the tee; there is water left and the entire fairway in front of you. Yet your attention turns to the place you don't want to go – the water. Now you fight it, telling yourself not to go left. Only one problem, this isn't the solution.

If I say to you don't think of an elephant, chances are you are thinking of an elephant. You see the thing to understand is the brain doesn't really hear the word "don't". It hears the words after, so in this case "think of an elephant". Now put that into golfing terms "Don't go left". All the mind has heard is "go left". I know what my money is going on, that the ball will go left.

All we want to do is hit the ball towards a target down the fairway. Yet we are focusing on what we don't want to do. Imagine walking down the street saying "don't walk into the wall", "don't go in the wrong shop". This would never happen; we walk down the street focusing on where we are going. Golf should follow this principle. Fine acknowledge the trouble or the places you don't want go before the club is chosen but then once chosen the focus should be on where we want to go.

Change your mind set away from "don't go left, to "I want to go at that target down the fairway". Now you are focused on what you want to do rather than what you don't want to do. "Do's not don'ts".

"How did I make a twelve on a par five hole? It's simple. I missed a four-foot putt for an eleven."

Arnold Palmer

2. "Get it inside a dustbin lid"

Two fantastic shots have seen you put the ball on the toughest par 4 green on the course. Now however your attention turns to the 40ft putt you have. The conscious mind kicks in and you remember a great piece of advice you were given "Get it inside a dustbin lid". Love the idea but where is the fun in this? Chances are you play this game for a hobby so you may as well have some fun trying to roll a long putt in. Hold right there though because the last thing you want to do is race it by because you got over eager to hole a putt you may only hole once every 15 rounds. So let's go back to the "dustbin lid". Admittedly this would be a great result but check out the diagram on the following page.

If you aim to get within a dustbin lid and miss it by 2ft that is not bad. Now however, you hit the putt and this time with the goal of holing it and you hit an equally accurate putt by missing that by 2ft, just look at the result the ball lies in from the hole:

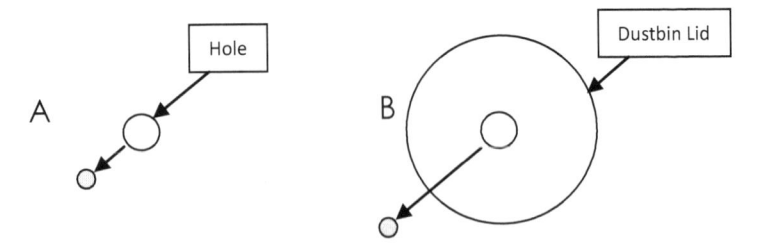

[Figure A: Hole with ball missing by 2ft] [Figure B: Dustbin Lid with ball missing by 4ft]

The above image shows the obvious result. A ball missing the hole by 2ft finishes 2ft from it as in figure A. A ball missing the larger target (dustbin lid) by also 2ft actually misses the final target by roughly 4ft, as in figure B, leaving you with the task of holing a putt that the tour pro's hole roughly 75% of the time.

Trying to put a ball inside a dustbin lid is easier than trying to hole it yet with that mindset focus can be leaked. The key is to heighten the focus without applying unnecessary pressure. So next time you are in this position plan to roll the ball to the hole embracing the opportunity that it may drop in.

"If there is one thing I have learned during my years as a professional, it is that the only thing constant about golf is its inconstancy."

Jack Nicklaus

3. "I must hole this"

Why must you hole it? You may like to hole it but wouldn't we like to hole all putts? Of course we would but golf isn't that kind. Those who work, have a family, in fact those who live, will come up against various pressures throughout their lives. Maybe it is paying bills, meeting work deadlines the list could go on. Those things are real life pressures some have. So now we have acknowledged these, is that putt you have really that important.

It is obvious we want to hole the putt but do we have to remind ourselves of this? No. Instead we suck the wandering mind back from the future and emotion of the putt, get back to present and the task at hand which simply put is find the line we wish to roll the ball down and roll the ball down it at our chosen pace. At the end of the roll there might just be a hole waiting for it. If not we tap in, walk off knowing we did all we can to roll the ball as best we could and enjoyed the opportunity.

"I never played a round when I didn't learn something new about the game."

Ben Hogan

4. "This lie is awful"

Nothing worse than a bad lie in the rough, even worse is a bad lie in the fairway. Hold on though we are playing a game that is outdoors in the elements on uneven ground and sometimes on a course that has been there potentially decades and centuries of years played by thousands of golfers. So guess what bad lies are going to happen – its part of the game. The reaction by many is to either let their playing partners know this or moan internally that the golfing gods are against them today. In perspective it is what it is and the one thing lacking from most golfers is the skill of acceptance. In my mind this is probably one of the greatest skills you can ever learn for this beautiful game and possibly for life. Accept the poor lie to allow the mind to focus on the task at hand. Instead what many do is go through their process physically but the most important bit, the mind, is sat in the past still moaning about the poor lie and guess what.... the result is a poor one. So next time your reach your ball in a poor lie don't blame the golfing gods, accept it, re focus and execute the best shot you can at that time.

"Of all the hazards, fear is the worst."

Sam Snead

5. "I hate this game"

I've heard this by so many, especially youngsters. However I have never come across anyone who is forced to play the game. It is a decision made by you and you alone to play this beautiful game. Yes you may be having a day that presents challenges due to poor striking and an out of sync swing but you still have two vital components you need to play golf – mind and body. Move away from solving your swing issues by making a conscious effort to make excellent smart decisions with every shot.

To play this game with an unsettled mind is not advisable. Yet so many play their round fighting so many things, the weather, playing partners and the game. Unfortunately they do not realise they are fighting one thing, themselves. Find peace out there by enjoying your environment and all that comes with it.

You don't hate this game you are just not firing on all cylinders today but how many great rounds a year do any of us have where everything is good. Not many so we better learn the skill to embrace our challenges on any day rather than fight them. The game is to be played not fought against.

> "You don't know what pressure is until you play for five bucks with only two bucks in your pocket."

Lee Trevino

6. "I hate this club"

Then change it. That's certainly one option, however, in a time where most of us have tested our clubs before buying them we become even more frustrated when the "damn club" doesn't perform on the course with a card in our hands. How can a club do this? Well news flash it doesn't. You do though. Your mindset has totally changed from the relaxed state you were naturally in when firing it down the range or into the net on the launch monitor. Now you have expectations of your new club and therefore put pressure on yourself to execute the perfect shots you were hitting in testing which led to the purchase of the club. What we want to do is recreate our state.

So get away from the outcome and expectations and get back into the process of the shot by choosing your target and executing a committed swing, a swing you were probably repeating in testing.

"For this game you need, above all things, to be in a tranquil frame of mind."

Harry Vardon

7. "I must hit this hard"

The rules of golf believe it or not are there to help us as golfers. One of the rules is everyone is allowed up to 14 clubs. Yet time after time you see so many golfers going all out with a 7 iron and more often than not missing their desired target. Keep things simple and move to the 6 iron. If you are an amateur, let's say off 12 handicap the chances of you hitting a pure strike to get the distance is slim so play smart and that way if you do strike it below average then the miss will not be as short as with the shorter club which most likely will also be wider. Even the best in the world you rarely see them choosing to go all out on a shot.

Take the extra club and swing within yourself and watch accuracy improve and the miss hit shots finish in a better position. You will find most trouble is short of the green, so why would you miss it there?

"A lot of guys who have never choked, have never been in the position to do so."

Tom Watson

8. "I hit it great in practice"

Don't we all? One of the best is when you hear people tell you they are shooting great numbers in practice rounds. Unfortunately however we are judged handicap wise and tournament wise by our competitive rounds. Yet why and how can we hit it so great in practice and yet so poorly on the course? Well the answer is simple; state. We are surrounded by states, states of people. Happy state, sad state, frustrated state, calm state the list goes on. We have to become very mindful of the states we create for ourselves because some can be very beneficial and others harmful. In practice be aware of the state you create. My guessing is you are probably in a relaxed and calm state. However some of you may start that way but move into a frustrated and annoyed state if you hit it poor. Are the last two states really good for golf? Not a chance and certainly not in practice because you are training yourself to get annoyed and frustrated at poor shots in practice so guess what happens in play? You got it you become frustrated and annoyed in play.

So next time you are practicing become aware of your state and maintain a consistent state throughout your entire practice session regardless of results then you may just see a reflection of this in play.

"Why am I using a new putter? Because the last one didn't float too well."

Craig Stadler

9. "I haven't got time to practice"

Single, no family and free you have all the time in the world probably which is great but let's get realistic, unless it is your job to play golf then you have commitments elsewhere whether it be family, job or other commitments in life.

We all know practice will help improve our game but remember this, it is not the hours but the quality of minutes. Take a few minutes to look at how much time you can commit to each week and work towards that. Whether it is 3 hours, 1 hour or even just 30 minutes, work to that so you become less hard on yourself for slacking. Most don't slack and would love to spend more time practicing but they just can't.

Once you have that time in mind then look at the areas you are most weak on. If it is chipping then commit a larger portion of your time to that area of the game with quality drills where you can record or see evidence of improvement which in turn will increase belief in your game. Even a 10 minute session can be beneficial if you have a clear plan for the session. It might be hit 20 chips from various points around the green and record how many finish within 3ft. That 10 minute session turns into a focused session with heightened focus over every shot rather than a session where the only focus lies in the first and last ball and the rest just get lost or become a ticked box.

"The mind messes up more shots than the body."

Tommy Bolt

10. "I was fine until the halfway house"

Such a common statement for so many amateur golfers. Some may say it's easy in the professional game because they don't have a halfway house to stop at. Well physically they don't but they could still mentally acknowledge they are at the half way stage yet they don't. Why is that? Well the halfway house is actually not the problem. The problem, I hate to say, is you. The halfway house objectively is a nice break to stop, sit down and maybe have a drink depending on the facilities available. However the majority of golfers choose this time to analyse how the front nine holes went and then try to predict what they could or need to do on the back nine. Believe it or not they are actually trying to play golf without a club in their hands!

Let's look at what happens at the halfway stage. Most amateur golfers check their scores with each other which then triggers a golfers mind into analysis and "oh wow that's my best front nine this year." Or "my word that is so bad". From this point the golfers mind now moves into a place we call the future, not a good place when performing. What are the signs of this? One word – predictions. The golfer almost plays the back nine in his mind highlighting what he ideally needs to do to achieve XYZ. He basically is awakening the conscious mind.

What we need to realise is that this time is not golf, as is the time in between every shot. This is a time you might sit down, have a drink, a conversation then go again. That is all it is. Therefore focus of the mind need not be on your performance but rather on something away from the performance. Would you discuss work on your lunch break if you could help it? I don't think so.

If you play with the same guys each week just ask them to not mention your score until after the round. Equally if you play with different guys each week it isn't unreasonable to ask them the same question.

In conclusion let's turn the halfway house experience into a positive one rather than an opportunity to analyse our performance and let a good round slip away or poor performance roll out into a worse performance.

We will enjoy the break from performing by having a good conversation with our playing partners or enjoy peace on our own before stepping to the 10th tee ready to perform the next shot.

"Golf is like a chain. You always have to work on the weakest links."

George Archer

11. "I missed so many putts today"

Newsflash everyone misses putts. The average percentage of putts made on the PGA Tour from 6ft is 65%. Those guys are good as well, yet so many handicap golfers get so frustrated when they miss from 6ft. What is one difference between the two types of golfers though? Well yes they practice more, it's their job etc they are obvious but what you find is those players we see week in week out on our TV's don't bring baggage to the putt, yet amateurs tend to. They bring the fact this is for par or this is to make buffer. A tour player brings no baggage just an acknowledgement that this is a putt and it requires two things, a chosen line and a good pace to roll the ball.

So next time you find yourself missing putts first of all accept you have and always will miss putts like the world's best do but then trigger in to choosing your desired line and your chosen pace then enjoy the opportunity of rolling the ball into the hole.

"Golf is a compromise between what your ego wants you to do, what experience tells you to do, and what your nerves let you do."

Bruce Crampton

12. "Come on let's hit a good first tee shot"

People watching, expectation levels high, practice gone great, these are just some of the triggers we take to the first tee. Of course we want to hit a great opening tee shot but in order to do this we need a quality process. What tends to happen is the average golfer is focused on getting a good result from the shot. Their focus should be on the process of the shot.

What I mean by process is acknowledgement of any nerves you may have by embracing them, knowing that nerves are a sign you are ready to play, this is followed by a quality shot decision leading to a great pre shot routine. The majority of golfers will have heard about pre shot routines and probably have one but there is a huge difference between a pre shot routine that looks good but the mind is wandering and one that engages the mind every time.

Wanting to hit a good first tee shot is what everyone would love to do but there is a bigger picture to the opening tee shot. That picture is that it has the same importance as any other shot you will have during the round. By labelling this shot as an important one will only pressurise you which in turn will tighten muscles which will result in off line golf shots. So keep that bigger picture in mind that every shot has the same importance whether the first or last shot of the round. Let's pick that smart shot to play, zone in on our target and execute the golf shot with commitment. If we do this we have done all we can.

"Every golfer scores better when he learns his capabilities."

Tommy Armour

13. "I'm always rushing to the first tee"

Wouldn't it be lovely to have all the time we want to warm up and get to the first tee? Unfortunately though for many club golfers this is not the case. Most have families, sometimes you may have been working or for others you had other plans before. Whichever you fall under the result is the same. You rush to get the gear on, maybe squeeze a few shots on the range then off you go into your round. I see it so often. Yet what you see at professional events is no rushing and loads of calm relaxed golfers.

Let's remain realistic though because finding that extra time to prep might be unachievable. If we can find that time, great, let's work out how much time we need and allow that. If this is still a no go then that too can still work. The key is to set the tone for the round. What I mean by tone is rhythm. All great athletes in any sport have great rhythm. They have different paced rhythms but they are their own rhythms which they have every day. Not just the way they swing a club, or run but in the way they walk down the fairway etc, they are always in their own rhythm and look in charge of the situation. This is something you can also create.

So next time you are driving to the club knowing you have no time to prepare as you want just slow down, even slow your driving to the club down, get your gear ready in a slower rhythm, walk to the clubhouse or pro shop slower and start to do everything at a smoother pace, what this does is trigger the mind into slowing down which is ideal. You may find it has an effect on your actual swing as well. Accept the situation you are in and take out anything you may rush, for example if you could squeeze 30 balls in on the range just hit 10 balls in the same time. If you can only manage 10 balls at a push maybe just have a few practice swings and hit some pace putts. Your goal is to step onto the first tee relaxed, calm and into your smooth rhythm.

"If you try to fight the course, it will beat you."

Lou Graham

14. "This is my bogey hole"

What is a bogey hole? I'm guessing you mean a golf hole where you have not had recent good scores on? If that is the answer that is the answer, it does not then become your "bogey hole". On the other hand it does become your "bogey hole" if you choose to dwell on past experiences whilst trying to perform in the present. Remember this, past and present as well as future and present do not belong together. They are separate. If you are acknowledging what did happen on this hole no matter how bad or often, you are in the past and therefore can in no way be in the present mentally. To be in the present would mean a sole focus of the shot in front of you with no baggage from the past.

So next time we are out on the course and walking to the tee of our so called "bogey hole", lets accept that was in the past and we are now in the present. Once in this place we make a great decision, go through our relative routines with heightened focus on our target and execute the desired golf shot with commitment - Job done. If we achieve this process we have successfully executed our shot. The result might be poor but if the process was good we increase the opportunity of the result being great.

"A man who can putt is a match for anyone."

Willie Park

15. "Whoever put those pins out today wants shooting"

Most golfers have played a round of golf, shot a poor number and blamed the pin positions on certain holes or even every hole. What we forget are numerous things and two of the most important things are these. One is it is out of our control where the pins are set and secondly and most importantly we don't have to go at the pins. This is massive. A golfer, generally one having a poor day will hit his or her approach shot into the green and be left in a shocking position with an almost impossible chip to the pin. The knock on effect is "well that pin is a joke". The joke is not the pin; the joke is the individual who got suckered into playing towards such a tricky pin placement. How many times have we heard Jack Nicklaus or Tiger Woods say they won most of their majors by making the least amount of mistakes. Just check next time you are playing, at the bunker nearest the pin, generally on the short side. It will have lots of rake marks in it from players being in there. Then check the bunker on the smart side of the pin. I bet it is smooth and generally unused. Yet this bunker is the one to miss in for the average golfer because it leaves the easier shot.

In conclusion next time you are faced with a tight pin placement play your shot to the smart side of the green, whether it is long, short, left or right. Finally remember that centre of the green never hurt anyone!

"Forget the last shot. It takes so long to accept that you can't always replicate your swing. The only thing you can control is your attitude toward the next shot."

Mark McCumber

16. "I've got the wrong club, I better hit it though"

Hands up who has done this. Not many will keep their hands down. We pull a 6 iron on the par three, feel the wind, tell ourselves it is probably 5 iron but think "ah I've got this now so I'll just go". Problem is we did that because probably sub consciously we didn't want to take more time to hit our shot in case our partners think we are being slow. Unfortunately however we now have to go in the bunker, hit the shot, rake it and get on the green. For the extra 10 seconds to change clubs on the tee we now have taken probably an extra 3 minutes to recover all because we had no discipline with ourselves.

We have fourteen clubs in the bag so we have no excuse to make do with what we have in our hands if we think it is the wrong number. Would you hammer a nail with a screwdriver knowing you should use the hammer next to you? No, you would get the hammer. That is exactly the same as the golf club decision.

"I never learned anything from a match that I won."

Bobby Jones

17. "I can't believe I missed that last putt"

Well you did miss that putt, but how you missed it is different to just missing it. The result was you missed it but did you do all you could to try roll the ball into the cup? If your answer was yes then that's it, you did all you can. You saw the line, you executed the putt with clarity in the mind but it missed. Process and result are two separate things. If you find yourself dwelling like this on the course just ask that question if you must, "Was my process good?" If the answer was yes then great move on. If it was no then you can take action by focusing well on the next shot. You should never try to make up for something because you can't. You cannot make up for a bogey on the last with a birdie on the next. That birdie is a birdie, that's it. It does not mean you made up for the last, you didn't you just birdied it.

So when you find yourself dwelling on the last putt, ask yourself if the process was good, and then look forward to the next opportunity to roll the next putt in!

"Golf is golf. You hit the ball, you go find it. Then you hit it again."

Lon Hinkle

18. "It should have been 72"

It's the standard line in clubhouses after rounds throughout the world. "What did you shoot Bob?" "Ah I shot 75 but should have been 72." The guys asked what you shot not what you should have shot. At the end of the day the number you shoot is the number you shot. There are always shots where you could have done something different, if that putt rolled in or that shot bounced over the bunker, the list goes on but fact is you shot the number you shot. Our performance lies out on the course not in the clubhouse bar. If it should have been a 72 then why didn't you shoot that number? You didn't because you either made poor decisions or executed poor golf shots. Instead of looking at what you should have shot look at why you shot what you did. Personally I would recommend you do this back at home once the emotion from the round has gone and you can then look at it objectively. Enjoy a drink with your playing partners and when in the car or back home just look at areas for improvement. This can set your practice plan up for the upcoming week potentially. Now you are being objective and looking at ways to improve rather than just dwelling and moaning about what could have been.

Duncan's Do's

1. Do enjoy your own company

2. Do enjoy every challenge thrown at you

3. Do accept everything

4. Do heighten your focus with a small target

5. Do get to know your playing partners

6. Do love your golf ball

7. Do smile more

8. Do learn something every time you play

9. Do play the game you want to play

10. Do have fun

ABOUT THE AUTHOR

Duncan McCarthy is an individual who is 100% passionate about what he does. Wanting to, in his words, turn potential into success for any individual or team is something that comes naturally to him. He follows no text book or set of rules. Instead he listens to every client carefully and implements what he feels is necessary to take that person or team to the next level by drawing upon his knowledge from his studies through University and his experience in coaching and life itself.

He has worked with individuals from professionals to avid amateurs through to leading businesses to help them gain an edge over their competitors on and off the field of play.

Ultimately Duncan prides himself on his undeniable passion and constant drive to improve and develop.